HYPNOSIS

THE BEST OF THE BEST

Inductions, Deepenings, Amnesia and Terminations

for your practice

HYPNOSIS
THE BEST OF THE BEST

Inductions, Deepenings, Amnesia and Terminations
for your practice

Emily Herrington, CCHt, CPLC, NLPP

Stacy Reed, LMT, LPN, CCHt

HYPNOSIS: THE BEST OF THE BEST

Herrington, Emily

Reed, Stacy

> Hypnosis: The Best of the Best, Inductions, Deepenings, Amnesia and Terminations for your practice

ISBN: 9781482674682

Cover photo by Kathryn Nee ❖ www.KathrynNee.com

Hypnosis – Therapeutic use

"May the blessing of light be on you
light without and light within.
May the blessed sunlight shine on you
and warm your heart
till it glows like a great peat fire."

~Celtic Blessing

Contents

Preface

When we each began our own practice, it took a lot of time and effort to find and collect solid, useful writings, and thus we began the timely process of writing our own material. Inside these pages you will find a book full of creative, insightful, relevant, and effective hypnosis texts for you to use in your own practice. Each induction, deepening, amnesia and termination can be easily adapted and changed to the circumstances of your subject. You'll notice that the writing, sentence structure, and punctuation do not always seem clear (or grammatically correct, for that matter), and this is purposeful, as each writing is laid out to be read just as they are written, with emphasis on bold print, pauses during ellipses, and brief stops at line breaks. This collection of inductions, deepenings, amnesia and terminations was compiled to assist you in providing "The Best of The Best" to those you serve.

"Until you are willing to be confused about what you already know, what you know will never grow bigger, better, or more useful."

~Milton Erickson

Acknowledgments

We would like to thank our colleagues and role models, especially those who have gone before us into this wonderful world of hypnosis. Those like Anton Mesmer, Milton Erickson, and the innumerable other unnamed professionals, who have been so eloquently equipped to deliver the message of help and healing through the art of the spoken word. For the endless sharing, the open-handedness of ideas, methodologies, and for the surplus of references, we thank you. It is with the help of these that we all, collectively, arrive at our own creative writings. We are greatly indebted to the availability of credible sources, the countless pages of tidbits, examples, samples and revisions that help us all to come to a beautiful place of poetic mastery that involves skill coupled with precise determination and expert motive.

Chapter One
Suggestibility

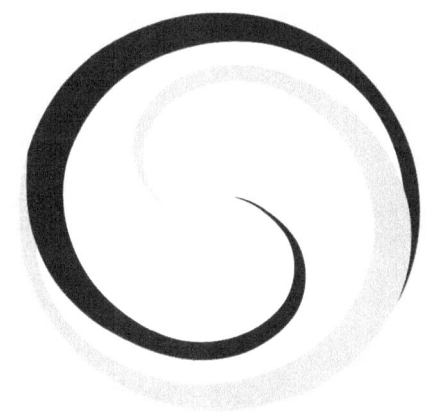

"He who looks outside, dreams; he who looks within, awakens"

~Carl Jung

Suggestibility Tests

Always do at least one suggestibility test with your client on their initial consultation so you can see how well they respond to directions and how suggestible they are.

Lemon Test

Don't read this script; learn it well and use your own words.

You're standing in the kitchen and as you look around, you see the refrigerator across the room. Walk over to the refrigerator and take your right hand and grab the handle to gently pull the door to open. As you pull, you feel the resistance from the seal, so you pull harder, and the refrigerator door opens, making a noise as the seal breaks. You open the door all the way and you feel a cool breeze hit your face and your body. You notice the light is now on in the refrigerator and you can see the contents inside the refrigerator. On the second shelf, near the back, you notice a single lemon. You reach in with your right hand, and as your hand enters the refrigerator you feel the cool air on your fingertips, hand, and arm as you reach in to grab the lemon. As your fingers grip the lemon, you feel a shivery coldness over your fingers. You pick up the lemon and begin removing it from the refrigerator. As you do, you notice the temperature change as your remove first your arm, your hand, and finally the lemon from the refrigerator.

You take your left hand and push the refrigerator closed until you feel the seal is secure. You walk over to the counter and set the lemon down on the counter. You grab a safety knife and slice the lemon in two halves. You pick up one half of the lemon and bring it up to your nose to smell it. Just as the lemon reaches your nose, you squeeze just a little too tightly and lemon juice squirts in your nose, on your lips, and in your eyes. Now, open your eyes and swallow. Was there more saliva in your mouth than when we started?

Sway Test

Don't read this script; learn it well and use your own words.

Put your feet together, with your hands by your side. Head up, and eyes closed. Imagine yourself on a large sailboat out in the ocean. It's a relatively calm day with swells around 10-12 feet. The boat rocks gently forward and backward. You feel the breeze as it blows your hair and against your face. Looking up, you notice the clouds in the sky and their beautiful shapes. You hear a noise off to your right, and turn your head to see the seagulls as they sing. You take in a deep breath, and taste and smell the sea air. It's so clean and fresh. You begin to feel the boat swaying from back to front and back to front. You hear the clinking of the clasps for the sails as it gets a little rocky... front and back...front and back. You reach out with your left hand and grab the rail as you start to lose your balance as the boat rocks steadily front to back... to front... to back... to front... to back.

Book and Balloon Test

Don't read this script; learn it well and use your own words.

Turn your right hand over and pretend I am placing the heaviest dictionary you can imagine in your right hand. Smell the old dust. Smell the age-old leather binding. Now, on your left hand I am going to tie a balloon with a ribbon and I'm going to let it go. You feel your left hand getting lighter and lighter as the wind pulls the balloon up. Your right hand is getting tired from holding the heavy dictionary. Now I tie a second balloon to your left hand and your hand gets even lighter and lighter.

As soon as you can see a difference in their hands tell them to open their eyes and see.

Clasp Test

Don't read this script; learn it well and use your own words.

Clasp your hands together in front of you. Clasp your fingers, and stick out your index fingers like Charlie's Angels. Now, separate the fingers, leaving your hands palm-to-palm. Now, I have a vice on your fingers and I am cranking it tighter and tighter and you see your fingers getting closer and closer together. Tighter and tighter, and closer together. You feel the vice crushing your fingers together. Tighter and tighter, and closer together.

If that doesn't work, then press the fingers tight and tell them to feel that because pretty soon they will be there again. Have them separate the fingers and they go back.

Chapter Two

Inductions

"The greatest discovery of my generation is that a human being can alter his life by altering his attitudes of mind"

~William James

Progressive Relaxation Inductions

Eye Fixation

This induction is written to be read as a "constant flow" of monotonous, slow speech. Very little change of tone is necessary.

Ok. I want you to focus on one object straight ahead of your line of sight. As you focus on this image, you are holding your gaze steady, you are not deviating your sight from side to side, or from top to bottom. You are focused intently on your object. Take a deep cleansing breath. Now slowly exhale. Continue to focus on the object without moving your eyes.

Now, this time as you breathe in, you are imagining your lungs expand to their fullest. Now, very slowly exhale and blow out until all the air that was filling your lungs has been blown away. Now you will only breathe cleansing breaths. As you continue to gaze, your eyes will begin to burn ever so slightly, your eyes will also begin to water, and your vision will gently blur as you give into the instinct to close your eyelids. As your eyes close, you have drawn the shade on the world around you. You are listening to my voice, and you are following me as I lead you to supreme relaxation. In the softness of your body, you are beginning to approach a place where negativity cannot enter. You are in the safest place you have ever been. Starting from the tips of your toes, you begin to relax. The relaxation moves up through your feet, to your ankles, and begins to envelop your body like the perfect blanket. As the relaxation takes over your legs, it begins to relax the muscles in your calves, your thighs, and your butt. Moving up, as the tension in your navel dissipates, your back and shoulders settle into the cushions around you. Your arms are becoming limp, and your wrists feel relief. Your hands relax, and as you take your next deep breath... and hold it, you will follow by releasing the breath and any remaining stress will be drawn out through your fingertips. Your neck is slack, and your head is supported only by the cushions beneath it without any strain. Now, as you continue to breathe slowly in... and out... in... and out, your facial muscles will become slack.

Now you can just listen quietly to the sound of my voice... and of course you'll be aware of all those other sounds, too.... sounds inside the building, sounds from outside... but these won't disturb you... In fact they are going to help to relax you, because the only sound you need to think about is the sound of my voice... and while you're listening to the sound of my voice you can just simply allow yourself to be as lazy as you could ever want to be.... Just allow yourself to be as lazy as you could ever want to be...

Top Down

Go ahead and lie back and close your eyes. Take a very deep breath.... just relax and let go of all of the days' tension. Relax and let go. Now, take a very deep breath, deeper than you normally breathe, and then slowly exhale... slowly... all the way down... farther than you normally breathe out. Breathe in deeply... and breathe out... just feeling the stress, strain, and anxiety drifting away... drifting away... drifting away... So effortlessly, just imagining that the stress dissipates into a mist and just disappears. With your eyes closed, you're very focused on my voice. Totally focused and totally relaxed.

We'll start relaxing at the top of your head now, as the relaxation pours down, over your face, and soothing you as it falls down over your shoulders... draping you like a warm blanket, giving you perfect, comfortable relaxation. Softly, tenderly, the relaxation moves down your arms... warm relaxation covering each and every finger... each thumb... as the relaxation falls down over your chest... moving down into your abdomen... wrapping warmly, peacefully around your hips... moving down slowly. Relaxation moving down through your thighs, your calves, and your knees. Then moving down into your ankles, penetrating into the arches of your feet... slowly, gently, massaging into each toe, and feeling the wonderful feeling of total peace and relaxation that now begins to take over your entire body. Every cell, every muscle, every fiber is totally and beautifully relaxed. Enjoying how you are feeling right now, embracing the serenity, loving every moment, every breath, each one deeper... and deeper... and deeper... as you give yourself permission to relax now.

Anti-Anxiety

*This induction is written to be read exactly as it is laid out;
short, concise statements, with emphasis on bold print.*

Now

as you start to **relax very deeply**

to settle your mind and give your body a opportunity

to **rest and relax**

you can **just begin healing**

by taking a few slow deep breaths

extending each breath out

into a **long perfect drone**

that can **wisk away any and all surplus anxiety** within

you

and just **exhale it all out**

as you **breathe in**

an energy completely capable of transformation

as healing flows throughout your body

filling your spirit

with a **peaceful**

immovable cloak

of **nurturing rest**

beginning at the tips of your toes

and even giving your toes a tingling in movement

and feeling a warming soothing awareness

begin to envelop around your feet

and up your legs, through to the bone

breathing effortlessly and fully

silky soft breaths

as that positive energy

wraps and entwines its way up your calves and thighs

like vines of relaxation

spreading and penetrating every muscle

every cell

as you allow part of your mind

to consider the times and events

when you've felt ever so luxuriously rested

and now you feel

beautifully relaxed and calm

how that energy can emanate to the muscles in the pelvis

abdomen

and spine

to just let go

release

memories of lying by a pool

the warmth of the sunshine on your skin

or a beautiful scene

from somewhere in a world far away

the flutter of butterflies

the smell of fresh, spring air

how your upper back and chest just know

how to relax very deeply

as you breathe in comfort and relaxation

and notice your head sagging

letting go

how there are alert and conscious parts to your awareness

and unconscious parts

and your conscious mind can just observe

whether your right foot

feels heavier

than the other

which feels the most relaxed

and the lighter one that's left

that's right

can be as it is

a deep, penetrating

floating sensation

with thoughts slowing

brow-line softening

facial muscles loosening

wandering

into

your mind's capability

to completely alter your body

through relaxation

to delicately unwind

the top of the head

the eyes

all by itself

like it does every night

when you drift off to sleep and dream

about things you desire

all the way down

to the deepest roots of your learnings

and understandings

that's right

and you know where

the rest of the peace

rests in the innermost place

or under

or deep within

your unconscious

to grow and learn

understand

while your conscious mind drifts.

Cabin

Ok, I want you to lie back and relax...moving around a little until you are able to relax... checking to ensure your clothes are loose and comfortable... that your clothes are not binding you in any way. Now that you are settled in, I want you to close your eyes and begin to relax. In just a moment, I'm going to ask you to take a deep breath... not just any deep breath... I'm going to ask you to breathe in.. into your being... into your essence. And when you take this deep breath for me in just a moment, I want you to breathe in through your nose and breathe in all the air that you possibly can... I want your lungs to expand... Your rib cage to expand... and your stomach to rise... I want you to continue breathing in until you are so full of air that you can feel the fullness... all the way up into your throat... I will then ask you to hold it for a moment... then to exhale... through your mouth... completely expelling all the air until you can feel the pit of your stomach.

When you are ready to begin (client's name)... nod your head for me. (pause until they nod their head). Ok great, so let's take a deep breath in... Breathing in clean fresh air... filling your lungs completely... Feeling your chest rise and continue inhaling until you feel you couldn't possibly take in any more air... now hold for just a couple of seconds... and release... Opening your mouth, exhaling and releasing all your tension with this flow of release and continuing to exhale until you feel the base of your stomach... That's wonderful. Now I want you to continue with two more breaths just like this one. Feeling more and more relaxed with each breath you take... as you begin to sink deeply into the cushions, feeling your body starting to give... Starting to let go... and starting... to relax. Breathing is such a gift you have and can so easily be overlooked and taken for granted. As you continue with your two breaths... chemicals and gases... are being exchanged within each breath... and when you breathe deeply... as you are right now... amazing neurotransmitters are being released. Neurotransmitters... like... Serotonin... Dopamine... Opiates and even... Oxytocin. You may know what these chemicals do... or you may not... It simply doesn't matter... as these chemicals... know exactly what to do and how to help you relax...

increasing feelings of euphoria... feelings of well-being... helping you to relax deeper and deeper... And even deeper...

Faint popping noises in the distance... a familiar aroma of burning Sandalwood or maybe Cypress Pine... Or could it be White Oak... as you turn around... you notice the raw cut lumber beams that run from the pine floors to the rough cut ceiling... wall to wall windows overlooking the beautiful wide mouthed flowing river. The sun is shining in and it is a beautiful... sunny... day. Apple cider smelting on the stove... Ohhh take in a big breath and breathe it all in. What's left of the early morning fire is burning down, and you notice it's actually... rather warm and toasty inside.

You walk out on the screened porch and sigh a comfortable sigh as you feel the warmth outdoors as well. You begin walking towards the edge of the porch, taking in all the magnificent beauty...Through the wired, filtered view of the screens, you are able to see all that surrounds the cabin... flowering bushes... fragrant flowers... lush green grass.... aromatic trees... the stone walkway.... The hum of the gentle, rushing river. The Gardenias and Magnolias are so fragrant that the aroma carries throughout the entire back yard. You can taste the fresh, clean air... What does fresh air taste like? You reach and grab the handle to open the screen door... As the door begins to open... it sings it's own song and rattles as it slings closed behind you... Over to the side... Could be to your left... Could be to your right... You notice a large inner tube propped against the shed. What color is it? Is it red... yellow... green... blue. Or is it another color? It simply doesn't matter...

You are so comfortably relaxed now, that... you... simply... don't care. As you listen to my voice, you become more and more relaxed, and as you become more and more relaxed, you go deeper and deeper and deeper. For the purposes of hypnosis, anytime you hear me state the words... deeper.... deeper... deeper, you immediately return to this level of relaxation and will then go even deeper... Deeper... and even deeper upon suggestion. As you grab the handrail and begin to step down the steps outside the cabin you notice there are 5 steps. Holding onto the rail and stepping safely and securely, you begin down the steps... Five... Very relaxed... four, relaxing even deeper... deeper...

deeper...Three... Feeling heavier and heavier... two deeply relaxed... one... complete relaxation.

Waterfall Induction

Sometimes when you begin relaxing into a trance, your mind might not completely focus on everything I'm saying. Most people still have some wandering of the mind occur, and this is completely normal. Just try to focus on each and every word that I say though, one after the other, and pretty soon, my voice will just fade into the background. My voice might be the voice of a parent, a teacher, or a friend... or my voice might be the voice of a guide or a healer. It doesn't really matter... just as long as you focus on my voice and focus on relaxing. The sound and pattern of my voice will continue to relax you throughout this session. Even if at some point you don't even hear the words that I say, your subconscious mind hears me, and it is to the subconscious mind that I'm speaking to right now.

Just imagine with me now if you will, that you are standing in a natural pool of water, at the base of a waterfall about 20 yards straight ahead. The water is only knee deep, and it feels warm and inviting as you lean down to swirl your hands into the water. Feeling the warm water glide through open fingers, and feeling the warmth of the sun shining down on your bare shoulders. The water is so clear, you can look down and see your feet on the sand underneath, as you take steps forward to walk deeper into the natural pool. Walking closer toward the waterfall, distant splashing from the water's movement sounds peaceful, echoing against the rock behind it. Approaching the waterfall now, about 6 feet away, light sprinkles of water splash softly against your skin, as tiny droplets decorate your arms with perfect little pools of shining light... becoming now aware of the distant sound of birds overhead...

As you sink down deeper into the soothing warm water, your muscles relax and you bask in this beautiful experience... the warm water soothes your tired feet, softens your shoulders and neck... all your cares just drift away, melt away into the water surrounding you. As I count from 10 to 1, you feel each and every burden drain away from you. TEN, letting go. NINE, feeling free. EIGHT, releasing all negative energy. SEVEN, going deeper and deeper into perfect relaxation. SIX, restful, peaceful, relaxation. FIVE, deeper... deeper... deeper... FOUR, giving in, embracing relaxation. THREE, finding the last of the stress and allowing it to leave. TWO, almost completely relaxed. And ONE, perfectly, peacefully, willingly relaxed.

Interactive Inductions

Arm Levitation

*This induction should only be used on seated clients, never lying down. This induction is spoken in brief, but melodic commands, matching the speed at which the client moves his arms upward.

What I would like you to do, before you go into trance and go into that place of supreme relaxation is to place your thumbs only, very gingerly just touching the tops of your thighs, with fingers out, your arms at an angle, in the air, and unsupported. Your elbows pointing away from your sides, just floating nicely there. Thumbs are just barely touching the fabric beneath them so that you can just barely feel the texture... that's right, thumbs barely making contact and now focus your attention on those sensations in the tips of your thumbs where they barely touch, where that floating continues, because as I talk to you and you continue to engage and to pay close attention to those sensations, a most interesting thing is beginning to occur.

Everyone knows how easy it is to adapt to new ideas when you are comfortable, and sooner or later everyone has the distinct experience of learning something new when they are comfortable. So go ahead now and allow that relaxed feeling to continue with your recognition that after a while, you can notice that your unconscious mind has begun to gently lift up one hand or the other or perhaps both. It may be difficult to hold it there just barely touching your thigh as your hand keeps trying to move upwards just a tad as it feels weightless, and lighter, and lifts upward almost by itself at times, while the other may seem to get heavier... difficult to tell the difference at first, but as you pay close, attention it becomes easier and easier to notice which seems heavier, and which seems lighter... and when you begin to notice which hand seems heavier, you may let it relax, and come to rest gently on your thigh while you pay more and more attention to that other hand... to that light upwards lifting hand that moves up a bit at times, and back down again, and then back up again, and after a while you may begin to notice that you can allow that drifting upwards to continue more and more upwards, lighter, floating upwards, as you allow that movement to continue on and on... an automatic movement upwards, as your unconscious mind lifts that hand, that arm upwards one step at a time... upwards and then gradually more difficult to tell exactly how much that hand has drifted up - to tell exactly what position it is in, and it may be difficult to tell when that slow, effortless movement occurs more and more rapidly, as it drifts up lighter and lighter, higher and higher. That's right.

(˜ ˜ ˜ ˜ Pause for upward movement ˜ ˜ ˜ ˜)

That's right, and that hand and that arm can continue to drift higher, and become lighter and lighter, but as you pay close attention you may begin to notice how they feel now, how tired and heavy they are as your unconscious mind reminds your conscious mind to pay more and more attention to that heaviness pulling down, and that arm can begin to drift down now as that heaviness increases, and it would be such a release just to allow that heavy arm to begin going down now. That's right, moving downward, moving it down now, letting it return to a satisfying resting place where it can relax completely, and you can relax comfortably as you, too, drift down with it down into a deep, deep trance, as your arm relaxes, elbows relax, and the mind relaxes as well, and you drift deeper and deeper as I continue to talk, and your hands and arms feel so comfortable satisfied and relaxed. That's right.

Eyes Closed and Locked

This induction should be used with the client in a comfortable seated position. You will need an index card with a solid black circle drawn in the center. Position your index card just above their normal line of sight, so that they have to strain their eyes upward. Use your own words.

Just make yourself as comfortable as possible now... and just look here at this circle on this card right here as you listen to my voice... concentrating fully on this card... without allowing your eyes to deviate from this circle on this card ...

Very soon, maybe even already now... you will become aware of how heavy your eyes become... it happened quite quickly... they will want to blink and that's okay if when they do... and perhaps you even allow them to become a little misty ... or slightly dry... and that's fine too... they can feel so weak and so heavy... droopy and drowsy... tired... and it would be so nice to just allow them to give in and close ... as I bring the card down slowly... past your eyes... past your brow... past your nose ... past your chin... closing... closing... and closed now. That's perfect... you're doing so well...

already you are beginning to feel comfy and so deeply relaxed. Now I am going to touch the middle of your brow with my index finger... right here. I am locking your eyes from the outside as you now choose to lock them on the inside... and as I count from one to five you will find them locking tighter and tighter:

One. Eyes tightly closed. Two. Locking tightly and sealing shut. Three. Sealing shut as though there is a line of superglue on each side. Four. The more that you attempt to open them the tighter they become. Five. Now satisfy yourself... try it out and find them locking tighter and tighter. Now allow that feeling... a blanket of relaxation... to flow down through your body... from the inside out... your entire body becoming loose and free as all tension flows from you and you relax deeper... and deeper... with every word that I speak.

Healing Blanket

This induction is labeled interactive because of the touch to the forehead, but touch is not required. Feel free to use this as a progressive relaxation instead.

With eyes closed, I would like you to focus... all your attention... on this area that I touch in the middle of your forehead... so that your entire focus, your entire being... becomes totally transfixed on this one point in your head... just one point... and then I would like you to imagine this place as a bright yellow circle, just a perfect yellow circle that fits just right on this point... seeing this yellow circle so clearly... so now imagine if you will, this yellow circle just staying fixed in this one place, floating there, becoming a part of you... a lovely energy of light and pulsating warmth... this circle has mystifying powers, giving you the sensation of warmth emanating from it... shining right there in that place... a comforting warmth of protection... the positive energy shining directly into your mind... as it just stays there... perfectly transfixed in this place in on your forehead...

So now I would like it if you would see this tiny circle begin to float above you (*break the touch*), as if it resembled now a halo over an angel... hovering safely above the top of your head... it might be six inches above your head, or it may be closer, or even a bit farther away... it doesn't matter... but it just floats there, shining it's brilliant yellow, still radiating warmth, now down onto the top of your head... and now, the shape begins to transform, the yellow circle is now slowly becoming a square... stretching and growing, growing and changing, as you realize that it's beginning to resemble a large blanket, just floating so effortlessly above your head... giving off more and more brilliant yellow light, more warm energy as it grows. See it growing, watch it transform...

This bright yellow blanket now begins to slowly descend, draping around your shoulders, your arms, gently swaddling you like an infant... Oh, so warm and comforting, so peaceful... the feeling of safety and security warms your spirit, warms your mind... and realizing that this blanket is so special... it contains healing properties... it belongs only to you... it has no limit on what it can do... So now, this blanket, as it hugs you gently, seeks out and destroys all negative energy... seeks out and eradicates any discomfort, and illness, and you want to completely immerse yourself into this positive, radiant energy... basking in the glow of this positive, radiant energy... knowing that its healing qualities have no boundaries... as you think of this... see it happening... SEE it happening... as the constant stream of energy... pours into your body... starting in the pit of your stomach, the calm, healing energy grows outward in a circular motion taking over your entire body.

Confusion Inductions

All Those Things

Use this induction with analytical or intellectually orientated clients. It contains elements of confusion and since it is almost impossible to resist, it works particularly well with those who tend to find 'normal' relaxation inductions uncomfortable, or tend to challenge the truth of hypnosis.

I want you to relax and get comfortable. Just allow yourself to be as lazy as you could ever want to be... listening quietly to the sound of my voice... and while you're listening quietly to the sound of my voice, start concentrating for a few moments on your breathing while I wait... breathing slowly and steadily, just as though you were pretending to be sound asleep... and what you might look while you're relaxing there...

Someone with your intellect will be able to use the power of your mind to see yourself as you must look relaxing there... and then use visualization and the power of your mind to do whatever has to happen to make you look even more relaxed... all the while, still thinking about your breathing, making quite sure that each breath in, lasts the exact same length of time as the previous breath in... and each breath out mimics the breath exhaled the last time... even though each breath in will probably be a little bit shorter than each breath out... or maybe each breath out will be a tiny bit shorter than each breath in... and while you're focused on your breathing, notice that the weight of your head starts to feel heavier... and still listening quietly to the sound of my voice...

And while you're listening quietly to the sound of my voice, it could be, perhaps, that you'll become aware that you've forgotten to think about your breathing... but that's all right, you can just simply start thinking about your breathing again while you're listening quietly to the sound of my voice, and what I'm saying to you here... and there is a theory, that most people can think of seven individual things at one time, plus or minus two.

So, that means that most people can think of seven things all at once... plus or minus two... so you should be able to think now of at least five things all at the same time, but choose now to only think about the things that I give you... the sound of my voice... the rhythm and pattern of your breathing... the weight of your head... and how you might look from the outside... and that's four things... so you can think of those four things while you're listening to the sound of the music that's playing in the background... so that's five things, now...

And I'm wondering if you can now think about those five things and then at the same time notice the sixth thing which is the way your feet feel right now where they rest... and perhaps the angel of your elbows... and so that's the seven things now... the sound of my voice... the weight of your head... the music playing in the background... they way you look while you're relaxing... and your breathing... and your elbows... and your feet where they rest... and I wonder if you can now add an eighth thing into all of that...

I wonder if your mind is powerful enough to think of seven plus one thing... maybe adding in an awareness of the other sounds in the building... and then just testing to see whether you can add yet another input to your senses, like the smell of the candle burning... so that you're thinking of NINE things all at once... that's seven plus two... thinking about all those eight inputs to your senses and then maybe adding an awareness of the way the muscles of your face relax while you're thinking about all those other things... the weight of your head... your breathing... the music in the background... how you look from the outside... your elbows... the other sounds in the building... your feet where they rest... the sound of my voice... and how your face muscles feel... The weight of your head... your breathing... the music in the background... how you look from the outside... the temperature of the room... your feet on the footrest... your arms and elbows... the sound of my voice... and how your eyes feel, how your face feels...

And of course, when anybody thinks of so many things, what they are really doing is chasing after those thoughts, one after the other... very quickly... so quickly, it feels as if you're thinking of them all at once... and in the circus this is displayed as spinning the plates... spinning one plate, rotating back around to spin another, using your mind to attempt to do all this at once... and that's why some people can think of only five things... because it's the limit of their memory... while others can actually think of nine things... And I wonder how well your memory is working as you struggle to remember those nine things... the weight of your head... your breathing... the music in the background... how you look from the outside... the other sounds in the room... your feet where they rest... your elbows... the sound of my voice... and how your facial muscles feel...

And now you can think how peaceful it will feel... when you simply allow yourself to think of one single most important thing... concentrating all your positive energy into that one most important thing of all... which is going to be so simple... to decide what to think of, now that you are going to let yourself to think of only one thing instead of nine... or one thing instead of eight or seven things, or two or four things, just that one thing, and that one thing is how good it feels to only think one thing... thinking how relaxed you can be now... that you're just thinking of how relaxed you would like to be... relaxing in your mind... and in your body... and in your spirit, no need to think of anything else at all... nobody wanting anything... nobody needing anything... nobody expecting anything... and absolutely nothing whatsoever for you to do except to... relax.

Left or Right

Clients who are very analytical or extraordinarily critical will respond well to the confusion induction.

I was like you once, and I know how odd or even difficult it can seem to someone with your intellect to recognize that you can make a beneficial change for me to have the privilege to work with someone like you, of your intellectual capacity... the pleasure... as opposed to some who never come here and don't sit right there where you are there, and even they... perhaps someday... with their eyes shut can be so weak minded... always appearing angry at the world and never affording themselves for even a tireless moment... to relax...

Those are the ones who scrutinize and hold onto the notion that they have no need at all to listen to what is said or not said... putting a value and purpose on everything... values that have no place... here... no purpose... there... as if they totally object to growing and learning sustainable facts that will help them to view reality in a different way... that will allow them to finally care... that they can care for themselves... honor themselves... and be comfortable, as well... It is so comforting too... to know that you have that capacity to use your ability in that way... to learn and to accept that it can be such a relaxing undertaking... to allow that sinking into a trance to happen effortlessly... without concerning yourself... as you try to be aware of all that is said... the precise definition of all the words... and of all those things that occur in your own mind... thoughts... or awareness...

You can know too that you can choose... to forget to choose to pay that close attention... or choose to forget, or remember to forget... things... all that happens... here in your awareness or not... there... or what changes... your experience... or stays the same... and what about the mother who tried to do what she needed to do, to be what she needed to be? She needed a place to go... She knew that she had been told the right way to go... to instead go to a physical place... go ahead and keep to the left for the first part... that's right... it's so easy at first and then take that turn to the right... that's right... not the left because what is right is to take a right... then what is left cannot be right until the turn that is next to that is left... the turn to the left that will be right that takes her straight ahead to the next place, the next turn right away to the left that is right... and if that turn is right... straight ahead, then she would be turning left onto the right road... or right onto the left road... and pretty soon... all that was left was for her to relax... like you... and be totally unconcerned... because all that was left to do now was to continue... right... on down that road that went up the river to the right of the old car on the left, and then go right and then left... to be absolutely right...

It really can seem to be too much effort at times to be so concerned about what is right... that can best be left to those who need to know that which may turn out to be that or not... or perhaps something else entirely... which could be right too... if that was all that was left... And I know that you will be only too pleased to remember that when you consider that so many things can be identical but different too... like you and I which can also be an eye for an eye... and then up and down or two plus two are four... but then what for... if not to give in and relax and begin to recognize

that you really do not know what is no here or yes there...
where to go... to where you can let go and allow those
things to occur in their own time... as you let go while
holding on to that new realization ... that what you know is
that which is... that there is nothing that you require to do
or not do as your ability allows you to be totally relaxed and
comfortable... as you recognize that what I say can mean *so
many different things...* It can be so easy to accept all those
things and to be completely comfortable and relaxed with
all that is so right... and be left with that train of thought
that could allow you to stay on track ... and recognize that
too was not worth the effort... that takes so much effort as
you try to remember so many things... and to understand.
NO need for understanding...

The 12% of your mind, the conscious of your mind can do
anything... go any place it wishes to... without that need at
all for you to be so concerned that your subconscious is
concerned ... with right or left... to hear all that is important
to you... standing out here... as you continue to listen to the
sound of my voice that drifts down with you now... into that
calm sinking... floating... drifting of thoughts and of

experience too... that can go so slow, *so quickly now*... as that relaxation that is yours becomes more and more... as you can allow the subconscious of your mind to take too... the guided responsibility for allowing your own thoughts and your experience into a quiet calmness that follows this... that's right...

When thoughts can be turning within the awareness... as the engine roars and the axis turns... all on its own... nothing at all for you to do... nobody to please... or to be concerned with at all, as you drift effortlessly down into that warm, dark place where nothing is left... but only what is right for you... to where your own inner mind waits too with those wisdoms that are yours and those things that needed the two.

Sensory Inductions

Butterfly Garden

I'd like you to visualize or imagine... just think about... a beautiful lush butterfly garden. This is a beautiful place, a place that is so vibrant and lush, it reminds you of a tropical paradise. This place instantly puts a smile on your face, and brings back memories of childhood, chasing butterflies on a warm spring day. And in places like this in your mind, there are only wonderful things happening. This is your private, special paradise, your private, beautiful butterfly garden.

You find a blanket waiting for you in a soft, green grassy area, lush and magnificent by a small stream... you hear the water coursing through, you're gazing into the beautiful blue sky. You're lying on the soft green grassy area next to a beautiful stream ... you're gazing at the blue sky above ... a cloud above appears to be in the shape of a heart, and you are filled with a warm, loving energy. You feel the warm rays of sun, as it touches your body. The sounds from the stream bubbling past you sounds like a melody, and the crisp clean air fills your lungs as you take slow deep breaths... with every breath you breathe, a soothing, tender relaxation approaches, getting deeper and deeper with each slow breath. Looking over into the hedges, you see a family of the most brilliantly colored butterflies that you have ever seen.

They look so perfect; they don't even seem real. You watch the butterfly family move among one another as if creating their own ballet. As they slowly move up and down, drifting and flying, gliding through the air, you watch and become entranced in their glory. Each movement of their wings brings you deeper and deeper into relaxation. So, as I count down from ten to one, you will feel your own body float and sway, rocking and gliding like a butterfly, deeper and deeper into relaxation.

10 – giving in to total relaxation

9 – allowing yourself unrestricted access to freedom

8 – deeper and deeper into relaxation

7 – soothing, deep, comfortable gliding

6 – down and down... and down

5 – watching the butterfly, becoming the butterfly

4 – feeling peaceful, feeling safe, feeling comfortable

3 – deeper and deeper, to the greatest recesses of relaxation

2 – deeper... deeper... so... deeply... relaxed

1 – you are totally relaxed, magnificently relaxed

Rain shower

This induction works best if you have a photograph of rain or raindrops on leaves, and can have the client focus directly on one droplet of water. If you do not have access to a photo, modify to use any spot to fixate on. I also love to add in the sound of a rainstorm in the background.

I'd like you to sit comfortably, straight up, with your hands flat against your thighs. Focus on this photograph. Slightly open your mouth, place the tip of your tongue behind your top teeth. Breathe very, very deeply on the inhale. Stop. Breathe in more. Stop. Slowly exhale... blow, blow, blow, blow, blow until alllllll the air is out. One more time, tongue in position, inhaling deeper than you ever have before. Stop. Pull more air in. Stop. Exhale very, very, slowly... controlled exhaling. And now, the last time, tongue positioned correctly, inhale all the way in, pull in more, pull in more. Stop. Hold. Release slowly. Now relax your shoulders and the back of your neck.

Focus on this one raindrop [here]. As you focus on this raindrop, I'd like you to focus so intently that you are trying to see through this photograph to view what is on the other side. Without deviating your sight from side to side, or from top to bottom, focus so intently, so strongly, so very, very focused, that you can almost imagine seeing through the photograph as if it was a pane of glass in a window. Staring... staring... staring... Continuing with slow, deep, rhythmic breaths. Relaxing more and more with each, clean breath.

Now I'd like you to imagine that you are viewing this raindrop through that windowpane. You are beginning to imagine the sounds of raindrops ticking against the glass.

Now, imagine that you are standing in that window, looking out at the overcast world ahead of you, and you reach up to grip the shade and slowly begin to pull it down. As you do so, your eyes close as you draw the shade on the world around you.

With eyes closed, you are listening to me, following my voice, as I lead you to ultimate relaxation. Relax your head, relax soft shoulders, relax arms and hands. Feel the warmth emanating from underneath your hands. Now notice that you would like to relax the rest of your body, too. Eager to relax, eager to give in to this blissful state of total relaxation of the mind, body, and spirit.

Imagine now that you are climbing into a large, canopy bed. The bed is covered in lush, oversized feather pillows. The mattress is perfect, exactly the way you like it to be. As you position your body, the down comforter comforts you as you nestle into the perfect spot, that spot that when you find it, you never want to move. You can still hear the sound of the raindrops cascading over the roof, knocking gently on the windowpane.

In the distance, you hear a slight rumble of thunder, and the repetition of the sound is mesmerizing. Waiting patiently for the rumble, sounding out that the earth is receiving the water it needs. As you think of the rain, you relate the earth's need for water to your need for relaxation, which you have found in this session. Realizing the importance of relaxation for your health and wellbeing, you now make a choice to allow yourself to relax deeper and deeper with each number

I count down. Hearing the rain, listening to the rumble, you accept this countdown as a very purposeful, very accepted process.

TEN... letting go and accepting relaxation

NINE... releasing any and all tension that was there before

EIGHT... purposefully relaxing

SEVEN... drifting into the sound of the rain

SIX... deeper, and deeper, and deeper

FIVE... giving in completely, effortlessly, to relaxation

FOUR... feeling whole, feeling complete with this relaxation

THREE... deeper, and deeper, and deeper

TWO... almost into the deepest state of alert relaxation you have ever achieved

ONE... deeply, totally, purposefully relaxed.

Secrets

Just go ahead and embrace relaxation... nobody wanting anything... nobody expecting anything... Nobody needing anything, and absolutely nothing whatsoever for you to do but to relax... I want you to imagine that you're just a bystander and onlooker of your own mind... Diving down through the levels of your consciousness slowly and effortlessly, on your own time... Reaching the highest point initially... the part that deals with the comings and goings of daily life... where you make decisions and surrender to your choices, a place where your perspective of the world is.... It's like a crowded New York City street... full of people busying about their lives...

And you are just observing, quietly, watching, and then, slowly, diving down... lower and lower... and lower... still in the conscious mind, not yet in the subconscious... down to the part where things are half heard, half remembered... partly realized... the part where things are constructed before they really begin to transform into something deep and meaningful for you... this is like a lower floor, the stockroom maybe of a department store... the floor, perhaps, where everything is unpacked and made ready for distribution... And you just continue to carry on, drifting deeper and deeper... down... lower and lower... down now into the upper portion of your subconscious... this is the part of your mind that adds flavor to your thoughts... that makes you like some things and dislike others... the part where spontaneous ideas and limitless aspirations spring from... sometimes catching you almost by surprise... the place where all that store's stock is kept.

And you just allow yourself to dive lower and lower... softly, gently, down and down... to the lower levels of your subconscious... as far down as you can go... to the part of your mind that governs how you view the world around you... this is the floor that's critical to your success, the most important place of all... where accounts are kept and campaigns are decided... and judgments are made. This is the part of your mind that controls how you feel... it's the origination of feelings like jealously and pride... anger and joy... fear and trust... and all the other emotions that create you into the type of person you are... this is also where secret thoughts and memories from even decades ago are stored... memories that are sometimes locked away so tightly that even you have no conscious knowledge of them... but even without that precise conscious awareness, they can distort your judgment and affect your feelings... sometimes insignificantly... but often causing all sorts of other problems... Now I'd like you, if you would now, to use your creative thinking even more powerfully...

I want you to imagine yourself at the end of a long, long hallway... sweeping away in front of you in a long gentle curve to the left... so that you can't actually see where it ends... but you know instinctively that it's totally empty... that you are safe and alone... and as you move along it, you see that there are doors set in the walls at different intervals... doors to various parts of your mind... and eventually... eventually... you find yourself outside a door with the word 'Secrets' etched deeply into the wood... you can see that the heavy door is locked, and requires a very large key... and you realize that this is the room where your secret memories are kept... This is the place where you store your secret thoughts and memories... things that have been stowed away by your subconscious mind as a way to protect you, because they once used to upset you in one way or the other... things that cut you deeply in your soul... things perhaps that terrified you so badly you simply couldn't bear to think of it... and maybe some things that you simply found so utterly uncomfortable you had to reject them... they're all memories from a very long time ago... and they can't touch you or harm you now... but your subconscious isn't aware of this... and it continues to take the responsibility of protecting you from them... and that responsibility is a great burden in your subconscious mind... and because your subconscious controls how you feel from day to day... that weight affects you consciously. But these old memories are nothing more than distant thoughts now... they can't hurt you any longer...as your subconscious can decide to simply let them go... so you just turn that key in the lock, hear it release, and slightly open the door... just leaving it cracked... peeking in... and you'll find, over the next few hours and days that you'll begin to remember some of these old memories from the past... some during dreams... some while you're awake... some of them perhaps randomly popping into your head when you least expect it...

and for every memory you recall, you'll find yourself feeling just bit lighter, just a bit more content... just that bit more happy, and fully capable of getting on with today's task of living....

Flying Rocky Mountains

This induction engages the senses and induces a floating, soaring feeling.

Okay, you are going to take five deep breaths. Each deep breath is going to relax you more and more. Now, I want you to take a very, very deep breath.... So deeply that you breathe in until you can't take in any more air... deeply and slowly... hold for a second... and... slowly let it out... all the way out... to the bottom of your stomach. Don't push it... just easily and effortlessly let it out. You are feeling more and more relaxed now. Now again... breathe in... fill your lungs to capacity... and a little more... excellent, and hold... now release... feeling your shoulders go down. Three more times just like the last. And... breathe in... deep breath... hold here... and let it all out... very good. Now again... take a deep breath... inhale... slowly expanding your lungs... until you can't fill them any more... and... release the air... slowly... that feels so good and relaxes you more... and more... and more. You're beginning to feel loose and light, it's a great feeling being relaxed.

Imagine that you have the ability to fly. That's right. You can fly easily and effortlessly anywhere you want. Picture yourself flying over the Rocky Mountains in Colorado. It's summertime and all the colors you see are vivid, bright and magnificent.

You see mountains of dark green trees. Flying a little farther, you see sides of mountains that are rocky with large, gray boulders. Looking below you see bright blue lakes, flowing rivers, and creeks. It is such a beautiful sight, and you take in a deep breath as you take in the majesty. Flying higher and higher until you reach a high altitude above the mountains, you look down and see the most amazing aerial view. You see mountains, fields, and lakes for as far as you can see. You then glide down to a lower altitude so that you can get a closer look. As you float down, you relax even more... and more... and more. The only sound you hear is the sound of wind sweeping past your ears. Relaxing as you get closer and closer to the mountains and the beautiful view. Now picture yourself soaring just above the treetops on a mountainside. You take a deep breath in to further relax and you breathe in the smell of pine. It's a delightful smell and this too relaxes you. There are a lot of pine trees, and although you cannot see the ground through the trees, you know that these fragrant green trees are very tall.

You continue to decrease more and more in altitude and you fly just over a creek that is at the base of the mountain. You can see the movement of the water as it tumbles over small rocks and you lower your hand and let your fingers tip in to the moving... cool water... as you fly by. You think about where this creek begins. Thinking about how this creek probably originates near the top of the mountain as just a little trickle. Far down into the valley, you can see down where the creek grows wider and wider... as it flows into a beautiful lake. You take a turn and steer yourself toward the lake.

The lake is like glass; perfectly reflecting the mountains that surround it. Next to this lake is a field of wildflowers. The flowers are red... yellow... purple and very bright even from way above. It's so beautiful that you decide to soar down to the field of wildflowers. You glide 12 inches above the pretty flowers, and as you do, you reach your hand down and brush your fingertips very gently against the blooms. You are careful not to disturb them. The flowers smell sweet and fragrant. As you continue to float above the field of flowers and the lake, you hear the sound of a bald eagle soaring above you. You stay close to the ground so that you do not disturb it. Its feathers look smooth to the touch. You enjoy flying around the Rocky Mountains, as the view is very relaxing and you have seen a lot of interesting things today.

As you float in the air, you relax your body. You relax your face, and you make sure your head is parallel to the ground below. You loosen the muscles around your mouth and jaw. You align your neck with your back, looking down and making sure not to strain either part. You put your shoulders back and your arms and hands hang loosely by your side.

You relax your torso as you glide safely through the air. Even though your legs are moving, you relax them slowly and powerfully. You focus on each muscle in your legs starting with your hamstrings and quads and you move down. You are feeling very good and relaxed. Your knees

are relaxed; your calves are relaxed. You allow your legs,
feet, and toes to lengthen and stretch as you soar in the air.
You feel very good as you relax and you continue to relax.

Chapter Three

Deepenings

"And, when you want something, all the universe conspires in helping you to achieve it."

~Paulo Coelho

Deep Progressive Relaxation

This induction is written to be read as a "constant flow" of monotonous, slow speech. Very little change of tone is necessary.

Now while you're relaxing there, you can just be aware of your body, aware of your hands where they rest on the arms of the chair, perhaps noticing the angle of your elbows and maybe sensing the weight of your head against the chair back. And, you know, that weight might seem to just gently increase as you allow yourself to relax more and more, just being aware of your ankles and feet now, on the footrest, and wondering if they will start to feel heavy too, as you relax. Thinking about your breathing for a few moments. Noticing that your breathing is becoming slower and steadier as you relax more and more. Slower and steadier, breathing so steadily and evenly, just as though you were pretending to be sound asleep. Breathing so evenly, so steadily, you almost wouldn't disturb a feather placed immediately in front of you. Letting your breaths come so effortlessly and slowly, so gently, that you almost would not even disturb a single grain of sand on a piece of glass beneath you. And as you allow yourself to relax even more now, I wonder if you can perhaps sense the beating of your own heart. Sensing the beat of your own heart, and just seeing whether you can use the power of your mind to slow that heartbeat down, just a touch. Just seeing whether you can use the power of your mind to slow that heartbeat down, just a little, so that you can then feel your whole body slowing down. Becoming lazier and lazier, because you've got absolutely nothing whatsoever to do except to relax now. Nobody wanting anything, not a soul expecting anything, so you can allow your whole body to continue to relax and become steadier and easier until it's just ticking over, like a well-tuned engine. Just ticking over, smoothly, easily, quietly, and comfortably, so that you can become gradually more aware of your whole self. Aware of your hands and arms, just sensing how they are now. Aware of your legs and feet, too. Again, just sensing how relaxed they might be, and wondering if it's possible to relax them even more. To be so in touch with yourself that you can actually get your whole body, perhaps, to relax even more, yet remaining totally alert, and noticing now how even your face muscles can begin to really relax. Relaxing and letting go of the tensions that were there, almost, but not quite, completely unnoticed. Just being vaguely aware of the skin and the muscles of your face settling, smoothing out, a good feeling, wondering just how long all that tension had been there, where it all came from in the first place, and then realizing that you simply couldn't care less, because you can feel it draining away from you now, and that feels good. And as you continue to sense the beating of your own heart and the absolute steadiness of your body's rhythm, you wonder at the fact that you are so absolutely relaxed and comfortable that you simply can't be bothered to even try to move even one single muscle, even though you know you easily could, if you wanted to. I know that you easily could, if you wanted to; but you simply can't be bothered to even try. Allowing yourself to just be relaxed, and relaxing even more now. As lazy and relaxed as anyone could ever wish to be. And I wonder if you can now manage to relax even more, even though you are already as relaxed as it is possible for most people to ever be, just finding the last tiny traces of tension in your body and simply letting them go. With each easy, gentle, breath you breathe, allowing every muscle, every fiber, and every cell of your entire body, to be as beautifully relaxed as anyone could ever wish to be.

Floating Down River

Use this deepening after the Cabin Induction.

Gently rocking and swaying as you float down the river. Rocking and rotating ever so gently... ever... so... relaxing. The cool water gliding across your buttocks as you relax in the tube. The water... just deep enough that you float easily... and... effortlessly. Lying back and letting your head tip in the water... Coolness running from your head perhaps all the way to your toes... Resting your arms and allowing them to dangle by the side of the tube... Your fingertips treading across the water as your tube expertly navigates... the open flow of the river. I'm going to pause for just a few seconds so you can enjoy floating down the river... Taking it all in... Enjoying this peaceful, tranquil and serene journey. (pause for a few moments) And as the river begins to travels around the bend... every gentle rocking motion... Causes you to become more and more relaxed, as you enter deeper... deeper and deeper... into a state of deep relaxation.

Long Relaxation Toward Countdown

Now, image yourself walking down the cobblestone streets of Spain. The stones beneath you are smooth and comfortable under your feet. The air is crisp and fresh. A warm breeze passes by your body on this fall day. It feels good and refreshes you. You watch as the sun catches the stained glass window of a huge cathedral at the end of the road. The bright colors glimmer in the sunshine and it looks like large pieces of confetti sparkling through the bright light. It reminds you of fireworks. Beside you, you hear a gentle rustling of fall leaves, as they tumble over the cobblestones around you. You look to your right to see the colorful leaves as they dance among one another. Then you take in your surroundings. You are on a street with beautiful, ornate buildings on either side of you, and you are transfixed by the architecture. Far in the distance on your right, behind the massive structures of the city, you can see a mountain, and you wonder how tall it is. As you continue to walk down this road, you can smell the fragrant scent of an organic fruit stand nearby. You enjoy this smell; there is no other smell quite like it, and here in Spain it smells exotic, ripe, and fresh. It smells earthy and natural. You decide to stop for a moment at an outdoor café for a hot cup of espresso. It tastes rich and bold. Beyond the Spanish mountains is the bright blue sky. It is a beautiful contrast to the greens, oranges, and browns of the fall. There are a few wispy clouds in the sky. They look like quick white brush strokes on a painter's canvas. Then you find yourself standing at the base of that mountain in a vast, grassy field. You come to an area with a large comfortable blanket laying there for just you. You lie down on the blanket and close your eyes. As you relax your head, every muscle in your face releases more tension, and in your back each vertebra that supports your spine relaxes into the blanket. Your steady breath is rising and falling with your chest. Your hips, thighs and butt relax into the plush, soft ground below. Every muscle in your body is relaxed. You are in a peaceful state. Your body is completely at ease. You have nothing on your mind. You enjoy how you are feeling right now. In your minds eye you now slowly sit up and look above at the beautiful mountain and sky. You see that the sun is beginning to set behind the mountain to your right. The colors of the sky are changing into shades of red, orange, pink and purple. As I count from 10, the sun sets closer to the horizon and you relax deeper and deeper with every number I count. Ten..... the sun does down just a little and you feel yourself relax.... Nine.... you are going deeper into a state of relaxation... you see the sun lower and you are feeling at ease.... Eight.... deeper still..... Seven.... you are feeling more and more relaxed as you watch the sun go down.... down.... Six.... you relax further into hypnosis.... Five.... the sun is another step closer to setting behind the mountain and you are very relaxed.... Four.... you relax more deeply... and more deeply.... Three.... deeper still.... you watch the sun go down.... and down.... Two... you are very relaxed and at the count of the next number you will be completely relaxed.... One.... you are very relaxed. You are feeling very comfortable. We will now focus on your subconscious mind to make changes and you will allow yourself to accept all the suggestions ... that I am about to give you...

Staircase

And I wonder if you perhaps can imagine a spiral staircase... one of those staircases that's black iron, seeing the way the spiral staircase goes down and around and around... and you can now imagine yourself on that black spiral staircase... and you can imagine going down and around and around on that spiral staircase... gripping the cool handrail... And as I guide you safely, you can count yourself down that curious, spiral staircase... and the first step is TEN... and the next step goes down deeper, NINE... and EIGHT feeling more relaxed and more comfortable... and SEVEN drifting down comfortably... then SIX down and down... really, really relax... then FIVE - deeper and deeper... and then FOUR... nothing is important... nothing is critical... you have nowhere to go... you don't have to do anything... you don't have to please anyone, you don't even have to think... listen... anything at all... and then THREE you're getting closer to the bottom... totally comfortable, floating... then TWO ... almost there ... going down... into some warm dark place... where your mind can just drift away... if any thoughts come into your mind just let them go... the ripples in the water fading and slowing... you can ignore them... they'll just go away... and then ONE... you're at the bottom... feeling really good... totally relaxed... and you can just allow yourself to enjoy that feeling of release and relaxation... knowing that everything's OK and you're OK... and there are no issues... nothing you have to do... That's very good; you're doing very well...

Sunset

Now, I want you to imagine yourself at the edge of a lake. Looking down, there are soft, crushed pebbles beneath your feet, and slowly looking back up, you notice how the sun sits just over the edge of the treetops. You see the most beautiful, lush foliage all along the waters edge. As you take in this beautiful majesty, you feel the gentle breeze on your face. As the breeze passes you, you catch the scent of exotic plants, and fragrant flowers. This same breeze creates a soft ripple in the water, and you hear it gently break into the soft pebbles. Just ahead of you and to the left, you see a brown rowboat sitting halfway on the pebbles, and halfway in the water. You walk over and effortlessly board the rowboat, and without any strain, the rowboat glides into the swell of the water. Your seat on the rowboat is cushioned, and supports your back so that you are completely comfortable, and then you begin to row with ease. You have no destination; you are just enjoying the simple, safe, and serene journey. With each row of the oars, you become more relaxed. Your boat drifts along the water with ease, and your breaths mimic the slow movement of each stroke. With the first circular motion, you breathe in for one breath. With the next turn of the oars, you slowly breathe out. You will continue this slow, rhythmic breathing pattern. This is your own, private lake. There is no danger. You are completely safe. There is no one here to bother you, or interrupt your tranquility. By now, the sun has begun to go down. There is an opening in the trees and as you recline in your rowboat you will be able to watch the sun as it descends. As the sun goes down, you will begin to relax more and more deeply, with each passing moment. Ten... the sun is slowly starting to set. Each movement downward brings you deeper and deeper into relaxation. Nine... you are feeling your body relax. Eight... the sun continues to drop, very slowly and steadily. Seven... you are even more relaxed now. Six... you are feeling so pleasantly relaxed. Five... your body and mind are embracing how deeply your relaxation is connected to the setting sun. Four... you are feeling wonderful. Three... the sun has almost completely descended, and you are almost completely relaxed. Two... the sun is almost out of sight, and when I say the last number, you will be in a very deep state of hypnosis. One. That's perfect. The sun has gone all the way down, you are at total peace, and you are ready to embark on amazing changes in your life.

Beach

I would like you to imagine that you are on a beach. This is an adults-only paradise. There are very few people here, and they are far, far away. Walking on the beach, you feel the warmth from where the sun has heated the sand. It is the perfect temperature... You see yourself relax... it is 4 o'clock in the afternoon... the heat of the day has already begun to disappear, as the promise of early evening hangs in the air. As you move closer to the waters edge... you see two lone palm trees, and between them is the most comfortable looking hammock swaying in the breeze. It is waiting just for you. As you approach the hammock, you sit in it effortlessly. It fits your body perfectly... your back is supported... and you are lying in such a way that you can sit facing the water. You hear the seagulls flying overhead... you hear their songs to one another... You watch the waves roll and crash into the shoreline... the water is peaceful, yet large waves still occur from time to time. You can see them swell and break, crashing into the sand. As you watch the water, you begin to notice the difference in the size of the waves. Most of them are small... every third or fourth wave is larger; and as you watch the waves... you begin to embrace the peace of your relaxation. With the rolling in of each wave... waiting for them... watching for them... there is ONE... and each wave brings you closer and closer to deep relaxation... closer... and now see a large wave, TWO... as you hear the crash see the splash... then there's wave number THREE... just watching... peacefully... feeling mesmerized by the natural turn of the water... pulling and tugging each splash back into the ocean... watching... waiting... FOUR... relaxing deeper... and deeper... FIVE... each wave progressively relaxing your entire body... and by number SIX... deeper and deeper... SEVEN... watching... waiting... peaceful serenity. EIGHT... feeling relaxed... allowing yourself to drift deeper as the waves are crashing... peaceful drowsiness takes over... NINE... you have now come to a place of innermost satisfaction with wave... number... TEN... you are totally relaxed... so peacefully relaxed... and you may continue to sway, as you lie in your hammock, as we proceed through this hypnosis section.

Ferris Wheel

As you continue relaxing, weightless, an almost floating feeling, you imagine now in your mind's eye, that you are on a very slow-moving Ferris wheel in the children's area at a fair. You've had a pleasant day, the weather is perfect, there is a crisp breeze cooling the warm spring air, you are wondering how many perfect days are like this one. Sitting in the red seat of the Ferris wheel you feel a youthful exuberance, as the movement begins to relax you. Watching outward as you see the children laughing and smiling, you hear the encouraging voices of mothers with their young ones. As the wheel moves upward and around, and back down again, the rhythmic motion pleases you. Letting your head sit back against the firm and comfortable place behind your head, you feel at peace and joyful as you relax with each circulation. Breathing in clean, spring air on the upward motion, and exhaling warm breath on the outward motion. Breathing in slowly and easily, softly and tenderly as you gaze into the clear blue sky. Soft wispy clouds occasionally peak into your peripheral vision, with the sun behind you. Turning slowly, up and down, round and round, up and down, and round and round. As you become one with the movement of the wheel, you are reminded of the rhythmic movement through life as you pass through each stage of your life, moving and changing, up and down through life's challenges. Up and down and round and round, feeling pleasantly content with total relaxation and you connect this experience with your own life.

Riding a Motorcycle through the Mountains

This induction is wonderful for men or women who are sports enthusiasts, or those who do not have exceptional fears of accidents.

Relaxing and letting go as you completely relinquish any hang-ups, taking slow, deep breaths, I'd like you to imagine riding through the Blue Ridge Mountains of Georgia on a red Harley-Davidson motorcycle. As you slowly, safely, and effortlessly take each curve of the mountain, your legs gently grip the frame under you and your hands firmly grasp the handlebars, as the wind begins to race past you. You are driving at a swift, but safe speed, getting lost in what is around you, and the process or riding. You feel as if you are one with the road, one with the machine that you control. The scent of the mountain tangles with the rush of the air racing past you. Focused, relaxed breathing as you inhale and exhale methodically with each passing turn. The intense sound of the wind has blurred out any sounds other than the hum of the engine as you notice the vibration within you, the result of rubber on asphalt. As you glance upward, you see the familiar eagle flying freely, a clear distinction between you and the flying sensation you feel here on your bike. Taking each turn leaning left...... leaning right........ leaning left...... leaning right....... Breathing in with the left....... Out with the right..... allowing the vibration to freely overtake your body, leaning left.... Leaning right. As the sun above you begins to descend into daybreak, dusk settles over you, relaxation is upon you. Peace surrounds you, as you embark on new journeys in your life.

Old House

This deepening brings to mind a feeling of health and self control.

And I wonder if you can imagine a big old house somewhere?... it's the kind of house that's been there for generations... strong in stature on the outside... warm and comforting on the inside... and somehow glimmers of light always seem to be shining down on that house at any given time... it's a happy place... there have been so many memories there... holidays and birthdays... meals and candles... Christmas trees and Easter eggs... life has gone on in that house for a very long time... people have grown up in there and moved on.... Generations growing and changing... they have left to go away to college, go into the military, gone to get married... and they have all come back... some with their babies... some with new stories... little children have grown up in the kitchen floor... drawing on the walls, happy shrieks of laughter... it's a lovely place... And I wonder if there is a place like this that you could go in your mind... someplace similar that's safe and secure... someplace that really belongs to you... a place of solace... a place that you can go to in your mind... where everything is exactly the way you want it to be... everything is perfect... a place where only you can go... and you can freely move in and out of that place... a place where you will always feel safe and well... a sacred place where you are healthy, fit, and strong... a place where you feel full of confidence and ability in every possible way... a place where you know who you are... and why you are who you are... and this is just the place you want it to be. And this special place...you can always come back to ... it's always here for you... it's always here in your mind... and in this place... you are strong... and healthy... and in control... because you are in control of your life.

Chapter Four

Amnesia

"When you make a choice, you change the future."

~Deepak Chopra

Fuzzy Mind

By now you are so relaxed, and your mind is so full and maybe a little fuzzy. The things that I said are already beginning to fade from your conscious mind, because it is so difficult to retain all of that anyway. You will not try to remember the words that I have said because they are in their best place in your unconscious mind. You will forget to remember my words, and you might also remember to forget the words you heard, but either way, you will know that it isn't necessary to remember all of them, because it isn't worth the tiresome effort.

Time

As you continue your relaxation in your own very special way, every breath you take is comforting to you, and now I'd like you to take note of your breathing. And I wonder how much you have paid attention to each of the individual thoughts going through your mind. And then you can become perfectly aware of how difficult it is to remember what I was saying exactly 7 minutes ago. Because just 7 minutes ago I was saying this or that, and you can try to remember what I was saying just 5 short minutes ago, which was shortly after 7 minutes ago, or perhaps you're wondering what you were thinking 14 minutes ago. But, doesn't it seem like too much work to try to think about and remember all of that? In fact, it seems that it takes a little bit more effort than it is worth, so I want you now to relax, relax, relax, and understand that it is not necessary to remember what I say when it is too much work to do. You can choose to forget to remember what I said or remember to forget what I said. The choice is yours.

Long Analytical Amnesia about the Conscious Mind

You have been aware of everything, and yet you have not been aware. You have been listening with your subconscious mind, while your conscious mind was far away, and not listening. Or maybe you think that your conscious mind was in that place far away, yet your subconscious mind was listening. When in a trance your subconscious mind is awake, and listening, and hearing all these things while your conscious mind takes a back seat and accepts the calm serenity of this reprieve. You relaxed comfortably because your subconscious mind took charge, and when this happened, you forget to let your conscious mind do all the work. Conscious and unconscious, or subconscious, as it is. Your subconscious mind knows, and because your subconscious mind knows, your conscious mind does not need this awareness and can stay back, and pay no mind, while your subconscious mind stays readily alert and in control.

You have exhibited great potential in your subconscious mind, which you don't have in your conscious mind. You can remember those specifics that happened with your subconscious mind, but you can't remember with any certainty everything with your conscious mind, because it is in our conscious minds that we do not store what our subconscious minds were designed to do. It's easy to forget, and what comes with forgetting some things, is that you can remember other certain things. Remembering what you need to remember, and forgetting what you can, or need to, forget. It does not matter if you forget, for the act of forgetting, you need not remember what you can forget. Your subconscious mind remembers everything that you need to know, stored there, and you can let your subconscious mind, right here, listen and remember while your conscious mind sleeps and forgets as you hear. Keep your eyes closed, and listen with your subconscious mind, because right now your conscious mind is not, and when you're listening very, very carefully, and particularly, your conscious mind will not mind what it forgets, because your subconscious mind will remember what it has forgotten.

Brief and to the Point

Sometimes amnesia does not need to be full of grandiosity, but rather simple and precise, taking just a short moment to drive the point home. After all, your subject is hyper-suggestible at this point.

Now, as your desires have changed, you are already having difficulty remembering what this session was all about, and it seems that the more you try, the harder it becomes... the more you try to remember what was said, the less you actually remember.

Short Distortion of Time

Even though this time of yours today has lasted for this time, your relaxation has allowed that time to become distorted, or has it? Were the minutes still ticking by, as we passed 4 minutes, and then 8 minutes, and then 28? Or has the distortion allowed an occurrence of time to be distorted throughout this time, as the clock crossed over 15 minutes, but what seemed like 5 minutes, or maybe it's more like 16 minutes. Either way, the level that you are at now causes a level of curiosity of this time, and afterwards, a realization of this time; however, at that time you will not remember all of it consciously.

Dreamy

And when you come out of this wonderful feeling so refreshed and so clear there may be no memory recorded of this session, like when you forget that one thing where the harder you try to remember that the more you forget don't you? Like when you've been asleep and you've had this amazing dream where when you wake up you just can't remember any details as they seem to vanish as you try to recall them while you can just remember the incredible feeling you're enjoying now like when you've been day-dreaming and you come out alert and you may not even care about that but just go forward from there refreshed and content.

Chapter Five
Terminations

"He conquers who endures."

~Perseus

Direct Command

In just a few seconds, I am going to guide you back up to consciousness at the count of three. As you listen to my voice, and come back up, you will begin to feel very comfortable, and as if you took a wonderful nap. You will feel relaxed, but your mind will be clear and you will be confident that your subconscious mind will continue to act on every word of what I said. Each time we go through your hypnosis, it will become more and more influential in your mind. These suggestions will be a part of you and you will begin to see the effects of becoming a stronger, positive, confident person. Now, as I count, you will begin to come up. One, you are feeling good, rested, and in a wakeful state. Two, you are coming up much farther now, starting to move, and anxious to open your eyes to your new awareness. Three, eyes wide open, you are refreshed, relaxed, and in total control.

Thoughts of Success

So now I would like you think back over all those successes you have had in your life... and all those people with good wishes towards you... and all those people who support you ... and all the other things you have learned today...   And bring that feeling of success ... of certainty... and focus now on your hands... and just become aware of your hands... I don't know whether you'll feel one hand tingling or one hand heavier than the other or... maybe one hand will move or a finger will move... but you will know that it has happened. And you will feel the difference that makes a difference... that habit is now in the past ... that's your guarantee. You now know you have finished with this. And so with that certainty in mind... and those phrases going through your head all the time... I am going to count from five to one... and when I get to one you can come back to the present... not just yet... when I count from five to one you will find yourself coming back ... and you will be filled with that certainty... and all the things we have talked about are so true... and you will just know that you are different now... in many, many ways and you may surprise yourself at how different you can be... how easy it is... so simple... it's actually simple... and that's a good thing... So, counting now... FIVE... FOUR... beginning to get feeling back into your hands and feet... THREE beginning to flutter your eyes and shrug your shoulders... beginning a new life... and TWO, you are getting ready for a big stretch ... ready to open your eyes, feeling good... and smiling... ONE - EYES OPEN... back to the present.

Directed to Sleep

When people use recorded hypnosis sessions in their own home, they very often participate in that activity as the last thing in the evening before bed. For this reason, it is reasonable to expect that after the relaxation of the session, they can drift off to sleep. This termination simply does just that.

And now, give yourself permission to just fade out into a deep, uninterrupted sleep where you can drift and dream about all the wonderful changes you are making in your life. When you awaken tomorrow morning, fully refreshed and alert, you will be adequately rested and your natural energy will carry you throughout your day, as these suggestions that I have given to you grow stronger as each moment passes.

Swift and Aware

Now, each time we meet together, here, in this room, you will relax more easily, more quickly, with a clear purpose, with a richer and more precise depth each time. So, this time I will sound off from the letter E down to the letter A, and at the letter A, I'll then say, "Fully Aware". So at the progression from E to A, your eyes will open, and you will be fully aware, completely calm, totally rested, relaxed, and refreshed.

So we begin.

E: Calmly and easily you allow conscious awareness to awaken

D: Each cell, every fiber, all nerves and muscles loose and restored.

C: Blissfully aware, head to toe, of feeling whole and complete in every possible way. Spiritually, mentally, physically, emotionally. Total bliss.

B: On the next letter, feeling alive, rejuvenated, calm and serene.

A: Fully aware now. Eyes open, big stretch and a full, deep breath.